1 MONTH OF
FREE
READING

at
www.ForgottenBooks.com

By purchasing this book you are eligible for one month membership to ForgottenBooks.com, giving you unlimited access to our entire collection of over 1,000,000 titles via our web site and mobile apps.

To claim your free month visit:

www.forgottenbooks.com/free1115264

ISBN 978-0-331-38215-0
PIBN 11115264

PRIVATE OUTDOOR RECREATION ENTERPRISES IN

RURAL APPALACHIA

U.S. DEPARTMENT OF AGRICULTURE   ●   ECONOMIC RESEARCH SERVICE   ●   ERS-429

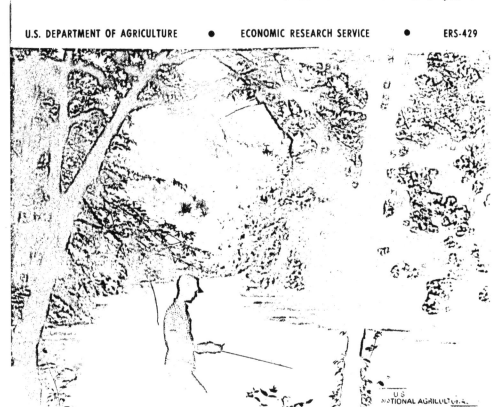

reel 5 1 1991

Washington, D.C. 20250   November 1969

SUMMARY

Most of the recreation enterprises that were surveyed were small, family-
operated, and supplemented other major income sources. Capital investment
specifically for recreation activities usually was small and often was undis-
tinguishable from that of the overall farm enterprise. A minimum of facilities
and services usually was provided.

Relatively isolated locations and managerial disinterest in expansion
helped keep these enterprises small. Occasional exceptions demonstrated that
supplemental enterprises providing larger incomes can be established when
favorable conditions exist. Managerial interest and capabilities often are
major limitations.

The analysis, drawn from a 1966 nationwide survey, included 35 campgrounds,
18 fishing areas, 14 vacation farms, 10 hunting areas, and 9 riding stables in
rural Appalachia. Half of the operators providing financial data reported less
than $500 of net returns from recreation sources in 1966. Only about one oper-
ation in six provided a net return of $3,000 or more annually. These tended
to be larger, better managed, better financed, and closer to metropolitan areas
than the less profitable ones. They also offered more variety in related
facilities and services and frequently were located in areas where clusters of
other types of recreation facilities helped attract visitors.

In general, the kinds and qualities of facilities found in this survey
have limited potential for expansion to meet increasing urban needs for outdoor recreation.

For the purposes intended, these marginal recreation operations can
provide supplemental sources of income and to an extent will help meet the
growing recreation needs of the public. Most, however, will operate on the
periphery of the vast recreation market.

Development of recreation opportunities on farms and other rural lands
has been encouraged by the Federal Government as national policy since 1962.
This study was undertaken to determine to what extent recreation enterprises
operating in rural Appalachia can help meet the growing urban demands for
outdoor recreation and provide profitable use of rural resources and employment for rural people. The 86 recreation operations studied were drawn from a
nationwide survey conducted by the National Association of Conservation
Districts cooperating with the Soil Conservation Service.

PRIVATE OUTDOOR RECREATION ENTERPRISES IN
RURAL APPALACHIA

by

Hugh A. Johnson, Judith M. Huff, and J.J. Csorba 1/

INTRODUCTION

Since 1962, the Federal Government has encouraged development of recreation enterprises on farms and other rural lands as (1) a way to provide additional income to rural families, (2) a use for unused or underutilized rural resources, and (3) a source of increasingly needed recreation opportunities for nonfarm people.

Both public officials and private investors expressed interest in opportunities for developing outdoor recreation facilities and services on farms and in rural areas of Appalachia. The contrasting ridges and valleys of Appalachia make it one of the most potentially interesting and scenically attractive areas in America. Some people assumed that improved transportation, lacing the Region with new highways, would provide needed access from urban areas bulging with people wanting recreation outlets. Improved access was assumed to help get potential recreation users and potential suppliers together in rural mountain areas.

SURVEY SAMPLING PROCEDURES

Five popular types of privately owned recreation enterprises (vacation farm, riding stable, hunting area, fishing area, and campground) were studied to provide insight into the situation in Appalachia.

Appalachia, as defined by P.L. 89-4, as amended, includes 373 counties in 12 States (map, p. 2). The sample was drawn from the 1965 inventory of private and public rural outdoor recreation operations conducted by the National Association of Soil and Water Conservation Districts, in cooperation with the Soil Conservation Service and various State agencies. No inventory was made in Virginia. Kentucky was eliminated, for sampling purposes, because the enterprises inventoried by NACD were too widely scattered for economical contact by enumerators.

_____

1/ Mr. Johnson is presently Agricultural Economist and Leader in outdoor recreation research, Natural Resource Economics Division, Economic Research Service, U.S. Dept. Agr. Miss Huff was formerly an Economist and Mr. Csorba was formerly an Agricultural Economist in the Division. This study was partially supported by funds from the Appalachian Regional Commission, under authority of Public Law 89-4.

APPALACHIA

Counties where enterprises were located

To derive a sampling universe of privately owned and operated rural recreation enterprises, the public, quasi-public, and closed-membership facilities were screened from the NACD universe as much as possible before the sample was drawn. Inadequacies in available information, however, still resulted in selection of several operations in the sample which did not qualify as privately owned recreation enterprises. Loss of possible respondents within the sample also occurred because enumerators could not locate the enterprises, the operators no longer provided recreation services, or for other reasons (table 1). This experience was one indication of the problems facing potential recreation enterprises in Appalachia: namely, that apparently few entrepreneurs who start recreation enterprises retain them over an extended period.

The limited amounts and poor detail of information that could be developed through the survey made it impossible to meet some original study objectives involving detailed analyses of the effects of location, management, and other institutional restraints on opportunities for developing viable recreation enterprises in the private sector. However, since even valid descriptive information about such operations is sparce, analysis was developed as far as the data seemed to warrant.

Campgrounds, fishing enterprises, hunting areas, riding stables, and vacation farms are the most common types of recreation facilities found associated with farms and farming areas. More than 2,500 of these types of firms were located in Appalachia by the NACD inventory. A sample of 460 enterprises was drawn. Analysis was possible for 35 campgrounds, 18 fishing areas, 14 vacation farms, 10 hunting areas, and 9 riding stables. Definitions 2/ for these types of enterprises are: Campgrounds--areas for tent, trailer, or pack camping, including transient camping; fishing areas--water areas having good fishing either owned by the operator or readily accessible to the users; vacation farms--a privately owned facility in which sleeping and eating accommodations are provided for paying guests. Guests may eat with the farm family or in separate quarters if they are housed in cabins or cottages and responsible for preparing their own meals. Guests may participate in some of the farm work and activities; hunting areas--an area of land or land and water for hunting wild game, including small game, big game, and waterfowl; riding stables--an area of using horses or other riding animals for recreation, including their housing.

DESCRIPTION OF FACILITIES

Small, family-operated enterprises are common among recreation businesses. Most of the management and labor are provided by owners and family members. The seasonal nature of the business, small size, and other conditions often make it possible for recreation to supplement or complement other family

---

2/ From instructions for conducting the inventory of existing outdoor recreation businesses by enterprises and activities, NACD.

Table 1.—Private outdoor recreation enterprises: Number in universe and sample, contacts, usable and unusable reports, rural Appalachia, 1966

Facility	Universe	Sample	Contacts						
			Total	Usable	Unusable				
					Out of business	Private or nonprofit	Could not locate	Other	Total
	No.	No.	No.	No.	No.	No.	No.	No.	No.
Vacation farm	108	75	75	14	1/ 14	—	15	2/ 32	61
Riding stable	156	71	70	9	15	3/ 22	16	4/ 8	61
Hunting area	250	99	99	10	8	5/ 26	2/ 8	6/ 47	89
Fishing area	1,621	97	97	18	18	7/ 35	2/ 26	—	79
Campground	394	118	118	35	12	8	31	8/ 32	83
Total	2,529	460	459	86	67	91	96	119	373

1/ Many operators reported that they take guests one year, but not the next. They were probably taking guests when the NACD inventory was taken.
2/ Includes those which could not be located and those with a variety of recreational activities unrelated to the specified recreation facility.
3/ Includes riding stables which have been sold and are now for private use only.
4/ Includes a dude ranch, horse farms, trainers, resorts, enterprises open only a few months, and one operating enterprise whose owner refused to answer questions.
5/ Wild game available on property, but private hunting use only.
6/ Owners do not charge for hunting, but, in many cases, accept gratuities from hunters.
7/ NACD inventory included SCS ponds built for conservation purposes. Particularly in Alabama and Georgia, many lakes were available for free fishing.
8/ Includes private boys or girls camps, those in business less than a year, permanent trailer courts, resorts, owners who were not available for interviews or who allow nonprofit groups to use their property occasionally or refused to answer questions. Four were actually in the business of selling lots for cabins and occasionally rented space to campers.

occupations and sources of income. The Chilton Study reported a nationwide
median capital investment of $64,000 for enterprises that provided full or
primary income. 3/ Capital investment for 26 percent of these enterprises was
$10,000 or less.

Recreation enterprises that supplement other businesses or other income
sources are the most prevalent. For those enterprises that provided supplemental income, the Chilton Study reported median capital investment of $8,000
and 44 percent of these operations valued at $10,000 or more.

Operating costs per unit of use often are high because the number of
visitors attracted to the enterprise is low. Volume of visitors depends upon
such factors as type of facilities offered (single or complex, day use, or
overnight), quality of facilities (rustic to ultramodern), advertising,
location, access, and personality of operators.

Location

Two factors usually considered important to the success of recreation
enterprises are location relative to population centers and the comparative
ease of access.

Access to many parts of Appalachia has been poor. This may be one reason
why recreation has remained a minor enterprise in the region. It may also
help explain why most of the facilities surveyed were found relatively close
to population centers. People simply do not travel the available mountain
roads into the hinterland for common kinds of recreation.

Of the 35 campgrounds, 28 were located within 100 miles of cities with
populations of more than 250,000 people. Most of these campgrounds offered a
variety of facilities complementary to the camping experience, including picnic
areas, fishing, beaches or pools, and refreshment stands. The remaining seven
campgrounds were at least 150 miles from cities of this size and tended to
provide only rental spaces for tents and trailers.

All of the 18 pay fishing lakes were within 80 miles of cities of at
least 100,000 population. Eight were within 70 miles of cities of more than a
half million people. Most of these lakes were stocked regularly with a variety
of fish. Operators located close to population centers often gave prizes for
the largest fish caught, and provided other complementary facilities such as
for picnicking or boating. Those in more remote areas tended to offer only
facilities for fishing.

All of the 14 vacation farms were within 150 miles, and 12 were within 100
miles, of cities of more than 250,000 population. A variety of facilities was
available at most of them. Included were boating, swimming, and nature trails.

3/ Private Sector Study of Outdoor Recreation Enterprises, prepared by
Chilton Research Services, Philadelphia, Pa., for the Bureau of Outdoor
Recreation, U.S. Department of the Interior. 1966. Highlights, p. 3.

All of the 10 hunting areas were within 80 miles of cities of 100,000 to 250,000 population.

All of the nine riding stables were within 80 miles, and seven were within 30 miles, of cities with more than 250,000 persons. Five provided riding instruction and conducted trail rides. Boarding horses was the major activity of the remaining four. These tended to be located within 30 miles of populous areas.

Land and Water Area

Recreation usually was not the major use of all land held by the operators. Farmers, for example, set aside relatively small areas for campground development or for use around fishing waters. Hunters could range over fields and forests without conflict with the primary land uses or, in the case of goose blinds, practically no dry land was needed. Similarly, horsemen from riding stables could roam over pastures, woods, and empty fields without interfering with usual farming operations. Horses being boarded can graze with other farm livestock. And farm vacationers benefit from strolling over farm premises or even help with seasonal work.

The reported size of holding--including both land and water--varied widely (table 2). The acreage developed for recreation ranged from a low of 41 acres for fishing enterprises and 47 acres for campgrounds to a high of 219 acres for hunting areas. Riding stables averaged 115 acres and vacation farms averaged 83 acres.

Within these averages, also, wide variations occurred. For example, two thirds of the fishing area operators reported less than 20 acres devoted to the fishing operation. Half of the campgrounds required less than 25 acres each and four in 10 required 10 acres or less.

Eighty percent of the land developed for recreation uses had been farmed previously.

Seven of every eight enterprises had water for recreation on the property, riparian to it, or otherwise accessible. Water areas included ponds, lakes, streams, rivers, and bays. Campgrounds and fishing areas averaged about 20 acres of water. Only riding stables seemed to have no ready access to water.

OPERATING SEASONS

The type of recreation enterprise and the kinds of personal services required affect both the season when operated and daily hours when personnel must be available. Nearly all enterprises were open 7 days a week during the season.

Most campgrounds were open 6 months or less. A few were open 9 months or year-round. Their peak season occurred in July and August.

Vacation farm----------:	14	80 - 472	14	83	2.
Riding stable----------:	9	1 - 460	6	115	1
Hunting area-----------:	10	80 - 1025	10	219	2.
Fishing area-----------:	18	6 - 900	17	41	19.
Campground-------------:	35	5 - 5000	22	47	19.

1/ Less than 0.5 acre.

Fishing areas generally were open for 6 months, from March 1 or April 1 to September 1 or October 1. Only two were open all year. The busiest months were May through August. Some fishing enterprises were open 24 hours a day.

Opening day for most vacation farms varied from March 1 to June 1, and closing day varied from September 1 to November 1. Four were open year-round but catered mostly to hunters during the hunting season. However, vacation farms are predominantly summertime businesses. The peak season occurred in July and August.

All of the hunting areas were open for two or three months during November, December, and January. Camping was allowed at two areas during the other months of the year.

Riding stables were generally open year-round, although major use occurred from May through August. Limited riding activity took place during the spring and fall. Boarding horses during the winter was the major recreation service provided by two operators.

OWNERSHIP, MANAGEMENT, AND LABOR

Individuals and families owned 72 of the 86 enterprises, 10 were partnerships, and 4 were corporations (table 3). The properties had been in present ownership an average of 11.4 years. Hunting areas had been held the longest (20.7 years) and riding stables the shortest time (6.1 years).

Owners managed 71 of the enterprises, 10 were operated by paid managers, and 5 by lessees. The owner-operators had managed these businesses an average of 8.1 years. Operators of hunting areas had the most experience (15.2 years) and riding stable and campground operators the least (5.5 years).

Six hunting areas were leased to clubs or groups where either the group controlled the hunting rights or the landowner controlled the amount of hunting on his land. Two were day-use deer hunting operations. Of the two remaining hunting areas, one was a pheasant shooting preserve and the other was a waterfowl enterprise where goose pits were leased.

The average age of operator was nearly 55 years and the range was from 30 to 83 years. Thirty-seven were between 30 and 50 years old, 31 were 51 to 65, and the remaining 18 were between 65 and 83. Generally, the more elderly operators were unable to participate in heavy work and the recreation enterprise often provided unexpected sources of additional income. For example, a 78-year-old man boarded horses on his property.

Many enterprises were part time, supplemental operations. About one-third of the operators were primarily engaged in managing their recreation businesses (table 4). The remainder had other full-time or part-time jobs. Riding stable operators were proportionately most numerous in the former category and most of them were over 60. At least four of the riding stables were primarily horse boarding operations.

Riding stable	9	9			6.1	6		55.1	5.5
Hunting area	10				20.7	8		60.7	15.2
Fishing area	18	14			12.8	17	1	58.1	9.7
Campground	35	29			7.9	26	6	51.3	5.5
Total	86	72	10	4	11.4	71	10	5	54.6	8.1

Table 4.—Operator's employment, average hours worked per week, and related data, rural Appalachia, 1966

Facility	Number in study	Principal employment of operators	Operators with other jobs		Av. hours worked per week in recreation enterprise				Family enterprise			
			Full-time	Part-time	In season		Off season		Yes	Husband	Wife	Children
	Number	Number	Number	Number	Number Rept.	Hours	Number Rept.	Hours	Number			
Vacation farm———	14	5	9	2	9	57.1	6	21.5	12	12	12	5
Riding stable———	9	5	3	1	8	65.8	6	43.2	6	4	2	1
Hunting area———	10	3	6	1	6	27.0	1	35.0	10	10	-	-
Fishing area———	18	4	13	3	18	26.2	13	11.2	14	10	8	8
Campground———	35	11	23	4	33	34.3	18	22.7	29	26	25	15
Total———	86	28	54	11	74	--	44	--	71	62	47	29

The reported hours worked per week on the recreation enterprise by the operator or his family appear to be unrealistic, particularly in view of the low tempo of activities in most of these operations.

Someone must be available during operating hours to receive guests and to serve them as required. However, this kind of service usually interferes only momentarily with usual farm and home activities at the particular time. As recreation businesses become more active and visitors are more numerous, they require increased time for labor and management.

Managerial and labor functions were performed by the operator or members of his family under most circumstances. However, 35 operators hired a total of 52 people for part-time work during the season. None hired more than five employees, even during the peak season, and only five hired one employee each on a part-time, year-round basis. Part-time employment was concentrated in campground operations where maintenance workers, concession stand operators, and lifeguards were needed. One operator provided part-time guide services for interested tourists.

A few isolated operators (five) hired one employee each on a part-time, year-round basis as caretakers or to do specific chores.

Part-time maintenance workers and comparable employees earned an average of $1.10 per hour. Part-time managers averaged $70 a week. Average weekly earnings of the part-time, year-round workers was $35.

CAPITAL VALUES

Average market values reported for land, buildings, equipment, and machinery frequently appear to reflect total value of these resources rather than the pro rata share properly allocated to the recreation enterprises. Thus, for example, the average value of land and buildings for vacation farms ($21,550) in table 5 probably overstates the proportionate share of use of the home, farm buildings, and farmlands. The same limitation seems to apply for estimates of equipment and machinery. Most farm equipment, such as trucks or haywagons, is used only incidentally for the recreation enterprise.

Conversely, of course, areas specially designated for recreation uses usually are entirely chargeable to the recreation enterprise. Campgrounds and fishing ponds with their associated land areas are examples.

The averages and ranges of values in table 5, therefore, appear to be a mixture, with the low point representing specialized recreation uses and the high side representing total uses. They could not be separated.

The inventory of supplies and other values appears to more nearly reflect investments in recreation enterprises. For vacation farms, this might include additional food, bedding, utensils, play equipment, and so forth. For riding stables, this item includes feed, horses, and tack. Hunting enterprises often provide dogs, ammunition, and special services such as cleaning game, gun rental, lockers, etc. Fishing areas often require stocking fish, fish food, boats, and gear. Campgrounds require garbage cans, firewood, light and water facilities, and some operators included items for sale as part of the supply inventory.

Table 5.—Market value reported, average and range, by type of enterprise, rural Appalachia, 1966

| Facility | Market value reported | | | | | | | | |
| | Land and buildings | | | Equipment and machinery | | | Supplies and other | | |
	Reporting Number	Average Dollars	Range Dollars	Reporting Number	Average Dollars	Range Dollars	Reporting Number	Average Dollars	Range Dollars
Vacation farm———	13	21,550	1,750 to 65,000	7	3,700	250 to 17,500	6	700	200 to 1,500
Riding stable———	7	20,700	1,500 to 60,000	6	1,400	400 to 4,000	1/ 2/ 7	7,000	200 to 10,000
Hunting area———	10	29,150	1,000 to 96,000	2	1,625	3/	2	4,400	3/
Fishing area———	15	24,250	1,000 to 85,000	12	1,650	50 to 10,000	5	400	50 to 1,000
Campground———	32	28,400	2,000 to 105,000	28	3,800	50 to 14,000	17	1,110	40 to 8,000

1/ One reported only supplies.
2/ One reported only horses.
3/ Data withheld.

In most cases, the operators were free of debt. The market values reported, therefore, appear to reflect net equity.

Half of the operators had made capital expenditures between 1960 and 1965. These included both expenditures for new buildings and facilities and major repairs to old ones, as well as, in some cases, those alterations made in order to enter the recreation business.

Twenty operators borrowed from commercial banks or received loans from government agencies. The rest financed their expenditures from personal resources.

RETURNS FROM RECREATION

The part-time, supplemental, and frequently incidental nature of these recreation enterprises is reflected in low returns received. Average net income gains ranged from $330 for hunting areas to $2,490 for riding stables (table 6).

Table 6.--Average recreation income, reported expenses, and net gains, by type of enterprise, rural Appalachia, 1966

Item	Facility				
	Vacation farm	Riding stable	Hunting area	Fishing area	Camp- ground
	Number				
Operators reporting---:	14	8	9	13	35
	Dollars				
Recreation income-----:	1,940	5,270	560	2,940	4,150
Reported expenses 1/--:	1,320	2,780	230	2,170	2,640
Net gains 2/----------:	620	2,490	330	770	1,510

1/ Includes property and other taxes, insurance, advertising, interest, utilities, supplies, hired labor, and other.
2/ Includes return to unpaid family labor and return to capital investment.

The apparent low returns understate the actual net income for some recreation enterprises. As with estimated land and other values (table 5), some operators apparently credited total taxes, total electric bills, total fire insurance, and other costs against the recreation business.

13

The fact that recreation enterprises are a source of income strengthens the justification for introducing such businesses. Fees paid for hunting opportunities may pay the tax bill. Earnings from taking guests on vacation farms may provide new home furnishings. Caring for a small campground may provide tasks and spending money for children. Boarding horses may provide supplemental cash and pleasant minor activities for elderly or partially incapacitated people. Thus, it is important to recognize that apparently small returns from small and intermittent businesses may tell only part of the story.

The array of returns seems reasonable when we recognize the nature of the recreation enterprises represented in this survey and the reasons why rural people participate. Average returns from hunting areas are lowest among the five types of operations. Their gross incomes are lowest and reported expenses are lowest. However, for the effort expended and capital investment actually involved in providing recreation services, returns may be exceptionally favorable. This type of operation, except for commercial shooting preserves, often represents income resulting from unusual opportunities. Opportunities for boarding a few horses or providing fishing opportunities frequently are of the same nature.

Returns from riding stables and campgrounds were highest among the five types of recreation enterprises. They reflected larger sizes of business through gross income data and reported a higher level of variable or operating expenses. Even so, several of these operations reflected losses or low returns (table 7).

Table 7.--Net gains or losses from recreation enterprises reported by 79 operators, rural Appalachia, 1966

Range in net cash returns	Facility					
	Vacation farm	Riding stable	Hunting area	Fishing area	Camp- ground	All
	Number					
Net loss----------	4	1	2	3	9	19
$1 to 500---------	4	2	4	4	6	20
$501 to 1,500-----	4	0	3	2	6	15
$1,501 to 3,000---	2	2	0	4	5	13
$3,001 to 4,500---	0	1	0	0	4	5
$4,501 and more---	0	2	0	0	5	
Total-----------	14	8	9	13	35	79

One fourth of the operations showed a net cash loss for the year. Another fourth showed less than $500 of cash returns over expenses.

Riding stables and campgrounds were the only enterprises where operators realized more than $3,000 for their labor and use of resources. These 12 operators were concentrating on recreation as a major enterprise. Their businesses generally were larger, better managed, better financed, closer to metropolitan areas, offered needed services, and frequently were located in areas where clusters of other types of recreation facilities attracted large numbers of visitors.

The three riding stables maintained 15 to 30 horses and provided riding lessons. The nine most profitable campgrounds appeared to be larger than average, provided both tent and trailer sites, frequently provided picnic tables and swimming facilities, and maintained related services used by the camping public.

Several of the 28 remaining enterprises earning between $500 and $3,000 had potential for becoming profitable commercial operations if the demand warranted or if the operators wanted more business. This was particularly true for several vacation farms and campgrounds.

Not all operators reported the same expense items and the range among estimates for any single expense category was wide. An impression of average expenses can be gained from table 8.

ADVERTISING

Most operators advertised very little. This lack of active business promotion is understandable when one recognizes that these people were catering primarily to clientele from the local area. And many were catering largely to repeat customers.

The larger and more profitable recreation enterprises were best advertised. Campground operators used three or four different media to advertise their businesses. They advertised extensively to attract tourists and vacationers. Most had roadside signs. Riding stables, on the other hand, used fewer advertising media and their customers were mostly from local areas.

Operators whose returns from recreation averaged $3,000 or less per year made little use of any type of advertising media. Some relied solely on word-of-mouth advertising to attract additional customers. Others used only 1 or 2 forms of advertising media, usually either newspapers or magazines. However, vacation farm operators generally advertised in 3 or 4 media. Only a few used signs at the entrances of their facilities. These commonly were of the small metal variety provided free of charge by soft drink or baking companies, banks, or other businesses in the area advertising their own products as well as the recreation facility.

15

Table 8.—Numbers of operators reporting cash expenses and average expenses reported, by type of facility, rural Appalachia, 1966 1/

Item	Vacation farm		Riding stable		Hunting area		Fishing area		Camp-ground	
	Reporting expense	Average expense	Reporting expense	Average expense	Reporting expense	Average expense	Reporting expense	Average expense	Reporting expense	Average expense
	No.	Dol.	No.	Dol.	No.	Dol.	No.	Dol.	No.	Dol.
Operators in study———	14		9		10		18		35	
Expenses						Number				
Taxes———	11	168	6	315	9	94	13	167	29	406
Insurance———	14	55	4	323	2	47	10	81	30	259
Advertising———	12	95	3	51	1	360	10	168	30	390
Interest———	5	138	1	810	-	-	5	932	12	615
Utilities———	11	386	4	173	2	21	13	184	32	324
Supplies———	12	603	5	2,152	1	150	13	1,212	28	440
Labor, hired———	3	129	4	510	2	150	5	592	20	1,031
Miscellaneous———	8	270	6	631	3	87	11	391	20	537

1/ Estimates for several of these expense classes may be for the total farm operation rather than for the recreation enterprise alone. Taxes, insurance, and interest are examples.

PLANS FOR CAPITAL INVESTMENT

Most operators who earned more than $3,000 were among the 35 planning further capital investment during 1966-67. Of these, 22 were campground operators. Half expected to spend $3,000 or less, while 10 expected to spend more than $10,000. Only 13 planned to borrow needed investment capital.

Operators earning less than $500 were primarily among the group who had no plans for further capital investment. They generally were satisfied with the present size and level of investment in their enterprise, were too old to attempt expansion, or felt that further investment could not be justified due to poor attendance or lack of customers. Some had difficulty getting long-term loans.

INTERPRETATION OF STUDY RESULTS

Many of the enterprises studied were small-scale and incidental operations manned on a part-time basis by family members. They were characterized by low capital investment, small total net returns, and limited facilities and services. These measures of financial success in similar situations reflect quality of managerial skills, intent of the operators, remote locations, and local trade orientation. In short, many operations were not intended to be major enterprises. Small scale enterprises can provide important supplements to family income and thereby make good use of limited capital and underutilized labor resources.

Few rational people would operate businesses to lose money. Yet it is obvious from the data that large total net income, while a factor, was not the overriding consideration in the activity of a majority of the operators. Many simply were charging for recreation opportunities available on their property. The small amounts of additional cash supplemented other income. Quite often, personal pleasure, congeniality, neighborliness, and other types of satisfactions or incentives weigh more heavily than the profit motives in explaining why people operate these recreation facilities.

Operators receiving more than $3,000 of net income from recreation had a variety of motives for being in business. Profit, however, was the primary purpose, particularly for campground operators. Riding stable operators also mentioned personal pleasure as a motivating factor.

Some operators who received low net returns were interested in augmenting their major income sources. Others derived personal pleasure from meeting people; still others were retired and wanted to remain active and continue using their personal skills.

Some enterprises may be open for customers one year, closed the next, only to reopen the following year. This tendency was particularly evident for vacation farms where use or nonuse of à few spare rooms by tourists is easily adaptable to the desires of owners.

Those few enterprises with net incomes of more than $3,000 were managed by experienced personnel. They were in good locations relative to population centers and frequently offered the only facilities of that type within 20 miles of others--or were close to other types of recreation enterprises attracting outsiders into the area. Their larger capital investments in facilities and their variety of services reflected a greater capacity for meeting the expectations of their clients. In short, the operators who earned more than $3,000 were more profit oriented and service conscious. Operators who had been in business longer than 5 years tended to demonstrate ability to accumulate capital for further business improvements. This phenomenon, although relatively rare, shows that farm recreation enterprises in Appalachia can provide substantial supplements to income--when circumstances are right.

UNITED STATES DEPARTMENT OF AGRICULTURE
WASHINGTON, D.C. 20250

OFFICIAL BUSINESS